INSECTS AROUND THE WORLD

ALL ABOUT NORTH AMERICAN BUTTERFLIES

EZ READERS

Annette Whipple

Creating Young Nonfiction Readers

EZ Readers lets children delve into nonfiction at beginning reading levels. Young readers are introduced to new concepts, facts, ideas, and vocabulary.

Tips for Reading Nonfiction with Beginning Readers

Talk about Nonfiction

Begin by explaining that nonfiction books give us information that is true. The book will be organized around a specific topic or idea, and we may learn new facts through reading.

Look at the Parts

Most nonfiction books have helpful features. Our *EZ Readers* include color photographs and graphic aids, a table of contents, a glossary, and an index. Share the purpose of these features with your reader.

Color Photos and Graphic Aids

A lot of information can be found by "reading" photos, charts, maps, and other graphic aids found within nonfiction texts. Help your reader learn more about the different ways information can be displayed.

Table of Contents

Located at the front of the book, this list shows the big ideas within the text and the page numbers where they can be found.

Glossary

Located at the back of the book, the glossary defines key words and phrases that are related to the topic. These words and phrases can be found in the text in colored type.

Index

Located at the back of the book, an index is an alphabetical list of topics and the page numbers where they can be found.

With a little help and guidance about reading nonfiction, you can feel good about introducing a young reader to the world of *EZ Readers* nonfiction books.

Mitchell Lane
PUBLISHERS

2001 SW 31st Avenue
Hallandale, FL 33009
www.mitchelllane.com

First Edition, 2025.

Author: Annette Whipple
Designer: Rhea Magaro
Editor: Kim Thompson

Names/credits:
Title: All About North American Butterflies / by Annette Whipple
Description: Hallandale, FL :
Mitchell Lane Publishers, [2025]

Series: Insects Around the World
Library bound ISBN: 978-1-68020-955-6
eBook ISBN: 978-1-68020-960-0

EZ Readers is an imprint of
Mitchell Lane Publishers

PHOTO CREDITS
Shutterstock: TigerStocks, cover, 1; Georgi Baird, 4-5; Natalja Petuhova, 6-7; jakrit yuenprakhon, 8-9; Sari ONeal, 10-11; Leena Robinson, 12-13; Oybek Ostanov, 14-15; golubka57, 16-17; Atosan, 18-19; Serg64, 20-21; nblx, 22; JoannaTkaczuk, 22; John_T, 22; Hannamariah, 22

Paperback ISBN: 979-8-89260-143-6

CONTENTS

Butterflies are flying **insects** with large wings. They often have bright colors. North America is home to many **species** of butterflies. More than 700 kinds live in the United States and Canada. About 2,000 kinds live in Mexico where it is warmer.

Butterfly wings are covered with tiny scales that look like dust. The scales overlap in rows. Scales help butterflies fly. They also give butterflies their colorful designs.

A butterfly's life begins when an adult female lays eggs on a plant. Butterfly **larvae** hatch from the eggs. They are called caterpillars.

A caterpillar eats plants. It eats and eats. It grows and grows. A caterpillar's skin does not stretch. To get bigger, a caterpillar must shed its skin and grow new skin. This is called **molting**.

After three or four molts, it is time for the caterpillar to hang from a wall, a twig, or a leaf. It wraps itself into a sack called a **pupa**. Inside, the insect goes through big changes. Long legs and wings grow. Eyes develop. This process is called **metamorphosis**. When the big changes are done, the pupa opens. An adult butterfly comes out.

Most adult butterflies only live for a few weeks. Some drink flower **nectar**. Others don't eat or drink anything. All are busy looking for a mate.

Most butterflies are active during the day. At night or when it rains, they crawl between blades of grass or perch under a leaf. Butterflies can fly when the temperature reaches about 60 degrees Fahrenheit (16 degrees Celsius).

An egg, pupa, or larva of some butterflies can survive the winter. But when it gets cold, some adult butterflies **migrate** to warmer places. North American monarch butterflies travel farther than any other butterflies in the world. They fly thousands of miles across the continent to warm places in California and Mexico.

Butterflies aren't just beautiful. They are important to nature and people. They spread flower **pollen** so that more plants can grow. We need butterflies.

WHERE DO BUTTERFLIES LIVE?

Butterflies live all over the North American continent. You can find them in these habitats.

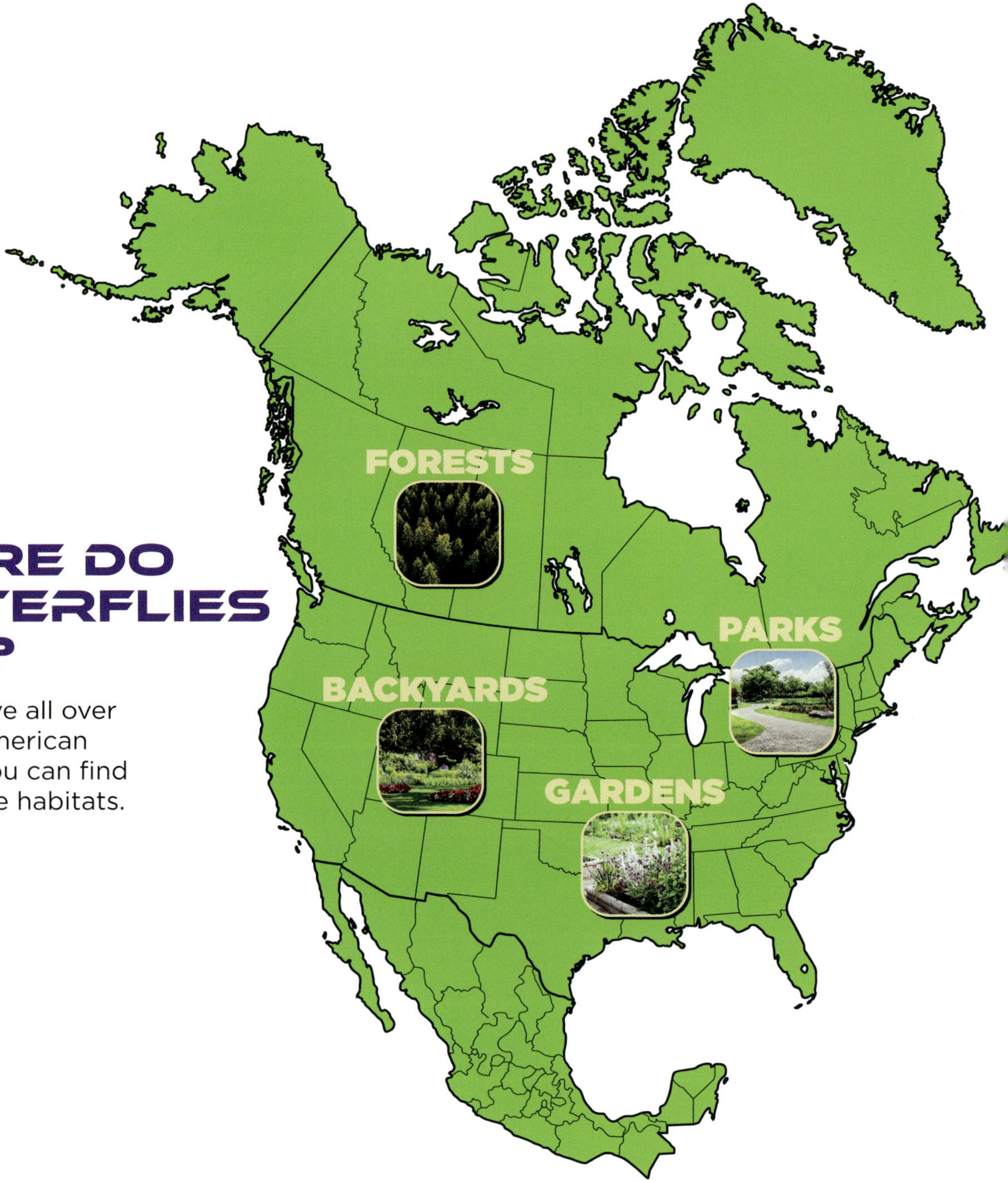

INTERESTING FACTS

- Butterflies can be as small as a thumbnail or as big as an adult's hand.
- Sometimes, caterpillars change their skin color when they molt.
- Butterflies lay eggs on plants that their caterpillars will like to eat after they hatch.
- Unlike moths, butterflies usually have club-shaped antennae.
- Butterflies warm themselves by spreading their wings and basking in the sun.
- Butterflies smell and taste with their "feet."

PARTS OF A BUTTERFLY

Antennae
A butterfly uses two antennae shaped like golf clubs to smell and balance.

Legs
A butterfly's six legs end in claw-like "feet" that can taste food.

Proboscis
To sip liquids, a butterfly uncoils a long, straw-like tongue called a proboscis.

Scales
Tiny scales make different patterns on the front and back of a butterfly's wings.

Wings
A butterfly flies with four wings that are flapped by strong muscles.

GLOSSARY

insects (IN-sekts)
Small animals with hard outer skeletons, six legs, and three body sections

larvae (LAHR-vee)
Young insects after they hatch; the stage of life between an egg and a pupa when an insect looks like a worm

metamorphosis (met-uh-MOR-fuh-sis)
A series of changes an animal goes through to become an adult

migrate (MYE-grate)
To move from one area or climate to another at a certain time of the year

molting (MOHL-ting)
Losing old skin so that an animal can grow larger

nectar (NEK-tur)
A sweet liquid made by flowers

pollen (PAH-luhn)
Powder made by flowers to help them reproduce

pupa (PYOO-puh)
An inactive insect that is changing from a larva into an adult

species (SPEE-sheez)
One type or kind of living thing; members of the same species can have babies

INDEX

FURTHER READING

Davidson, Laren. *Butterflies for Kids: A Junior Scientist's Guide*. Emoryville, CA: Rockridge Press, 2021.

Pryor, Katherine. *Home Is Calling: The Journey of the Monarch Butterfly*. New York, NY: WorthyKids, 2023.

ON THE INTERNET

National Geographic Kids: The Butterfly Life Cycle!
https://www.natgeokids.com/uk/discover/animals/insects/butterfly-life-cycle
Learn all about the fascinating transformation from caterpillar to butterfly.

Smithsonian Gardens: About Butterflies
https://gardens.si.edu/learn/for-educators/cultivating-habitat/butterfly-gardening/about-butterflies
Learn about butterfly habitats, life cycles, and more!